Tiny House Parking

How to Find Safe, Practical, and Affordable Land For Your Tiny House

By Ethan Waldman

thetinyhouse.net

Tiny House Parking by Ethan Waldman

None of the information in this book should be considered legal advice. Check with the proper authorities in these matters before you commit to any building project. The author is not responsible for your decisions or for the outcomes of actions that you take as a result of reading this book.

Free Bonus!

Download my eBook: *Before You Build: 30 Questions You Must Ask While Planning Your Tiny House*

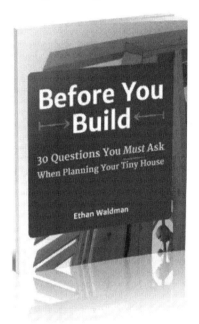

Want to get started planning your tiny house right away, but not sure where to start?

Download this free eBook to start answering the questions that will get your tiny house off the ground!

In This eBook, You'll Learn:

- How to stop ogling tiny house pictures on Facebook and start actually planning your tiny house today
- How to avoid the mistakes that I made and save yourself a lot of time and money
- The three systems every tiny house needs and how to design them
- How to stay organized as you research designs, materials, and techniques
- Where to go for even more resources to get your tiny house underway

tinyhouseparkingbook.com/beforeyoubuild

Table of Contents

Part 1:
The Tiny House Landscape

Introduction

Welcome to *Tiny House Parking*! I'm glad you're here.

When I published *Tiny House Decisions* (thetinyhouse.net/tiny-house-decisions/) in September of 2014, I was amazed by how many people were interested in what I had to say. I still receive daily questions that run the gamut of tiny house planning and building questions.

By far the most common theme I have seen in those questions relates to how and where to find land for your tiny house. That's what I mean by "tiny house parking," by the way: finding a location for your tiny house, whether it's on wheels or a foundation. This isn't just a book for people building tiny houses on wheels!

Tiny House Decisions is focused almost exclusively on making the choices that will help your tiny house be the right house for you (systems, utilities, building materials, etc.), though, and not as much about *where* you can put your tiny house.

The book you are reading now is a direct result of the many thoughtful questions I've received from readers, all of which were some form of "how do I get land for my tiny house?" In the following pages, I'll answer the following questions and more:

- Where can I put a tiny house?
- Where can I legally build a tiny house?
- Will it be legal to live in my tiny house?
- How do I find landowners willing to let me rent a place for my tiny house?

Also: Don't forget to download my free resource, 30 Questions You Must Ask While Planning Your Tiny House. If this book answers the "where" question, the free ebook above helps you identify the "what". It's a wonderful introduction to all the decisions you'll need to make about your tiny house *in addition* to figuring out the where to park it. tinyhouseparkingbook.com/beforeyoubuild

All right, on with *Tiny House Parking*!

A Brief Rant

As the tiny house movement gains in popularity, it's spreading around the United States and the rest of the world. What was once a small fringe movement in Northern California now has at least two reality television shows, its own conference, and hundreds of companies that offer pre-built units, workshops, plans, and more.

Even more importantly, what started out as a few bloggers sharing their progress online has grown substantially: You can literally find a new blog or Instagram feed documenting a tiny house build every day. I love the open and sharing spirit of the many online tiny house communities and am active in them myself.

There's a serious gap in all the tiny house coverage, though. We focus on the people who build tiny houses, the particulars of their tiny house designs, and their reasons for choosing the tiny house lifestyle. There's nothing wrong with those things, of course, but emphasizing them doesn't make it easier for aspiring tiny house builders to follow in the footsteps of the people in the spotlight. To realize your own tiny house dreams, you also need to know where people are living in their tiny houses and how.

People are still building tiny houses for a huge variety of reasons, but one of the main reasons cited early on was that building a tiny house was a way of circumventing (and in some cases calling attention to) the things that were so wrong in the American housing market: the runaway growth in the average home size, and the consumerism, debt, and other issues that arise as a result of this. Living in a tiny house in some places is expressly against some law or another, and that is precisely why people were doing it: to call attention to the system that seemed not to be serving them. I know, it all sounds pretty political.

This outright rejection of the norm is still the reason that many younger people are building tiny houses, but it would be a mistake to believe that the issues targeted by the tiny house movement have been solved. Not by a long shot. In our democracy, legal changes happen very slowly, and it's up to each town to decide what kinds of structures are and are not legal to inhabit.

Not to get all serious on you so soon, but just because you see tiny houses everywhere now, that doesn't mean that they aren't still on the fringe of what *most* people consider normal and what most towns consider to be legal. Despite their increased visibility, tiny houses are still in a legal grey area.

It is my hope that *Tiny House Parking* helps you understand what questions to ask, and evaluate where you fit within the (often) legal grey area that tiny houses inhabit. And that's the end of my rant!

My Story

When I first started building my tiny house, I didn't even want to think about where I would put it. What if I couldn't find anywhere to park it? What if the local zoning administrator found out about my house and asked me to move? I just knew that I wanted to stay in Vermont, but I had so many worries that it was easier not to think about tiny house parking.

My first indication that there was some risk involved with living in a tiny house came while reading Jonathan's harrowing account of essentially getting kicked off his land (tinyhouseparkingbook.com/jonathan). His story haunted my most anxious thoughts. I told myself that this couldn't happen to me, but still, I worried.

I decided that I would wait until the house was looking more like a house (instead of just a pile of lumber on a trailer) to start asking people about parking. My theory was that if they could just *see* how adorable and classy my tiny house was going to look, they'd be much more open to letting me park it on their land.

Luckily, I didn't have too much time or energy to obsess about this. I was far too occupied with the process of planning and building the house itself.

My initial plan was to park the house on my parents' land, behind a stand of trees, so it would be hidden from the road and also out of view of their house. They were willing and excited to have me as their neighbor. However, something didn't feel right about the idea that I would simply live in my parents' backyard.

I broadened my search, but I didn't have to go too far. My cousins, who also live in Vermont, own a small piece of property adjacent to their own. Even better, the property used to have a small cabin on it that was demolished, meaning a septic system and electrical hookups were still present. All it was missing was a house. I offered to pay them a bit of rent and to maintain the property for them in exchange for living there. They didn't hesitate to accept my offer. My tiny house had found its first official home.

It's true my own story didn't give me much first-hand experience with the nightmare that tiny house parking can be. It's not necessarily typical of the search for a place to park a tiny house. That's partly to do with my lifestyle preferences: For instance, I choose to live in a rural area because I enjoy the natural beauty, the lack of traffic, and all the open space that comes with living in such a place. However, if I wanted to live in a more densely populated area (as many people do), finding land would probably have been a little trickier.

I am, however, an active member of the tiny house community. I've done more than my share of interviewing other tiny house dwellers, reading stories, and researching zoning and other legal issues. Doing so has left me both grateful my own search was easy -- and eager to help others identify and avoid the common pitfalls so that they, too, can live their tiny house dreams.

The Problem with Finding Land

Why is it so hard to find land? After all, whether you're going with wheels or a foundation, renting or buying space, the needs of a tiny house are relatively few. This simple question has a whole range of answers. In truth, it's actually not all that difficult to find land, but it *is* difficult to find land that's:

- Within your budget
- Owned by someone willing to let you park a tiny house on it (if you'll be renting)
- In a location that allows tiny houses, that would give you special permission for a tiny house, or where a tiny house could be hidden (so you could go "under the radar")

Budget is an individual thing and not one I can really help with in this book, so I won't dwell on it. My top tip for finding affordable land, though, is that land typically gets cheaper the further you get from an urban center. For example, a small lot in Burlington, Vermont, can go for as much as $200,000, but if you're willing to drive an hour or so out of town, you can get a large piece of land for well under $100,000.

The second issue is usually the least problematic. The majority of tiny house dwellers I know whose homes are on wheels park in someone else's back yard and either pay rent, trade services, or offer some combination of the two. I'll connect you with lots of resources for finding the right landowner later in this book.

The last issue is the biggest: Finding a place where it's one hundred percent legal to live in a tiny house is nearly impossible. As I mentioned in the introduction, tiny houses are a very new challenge to the building and zoning legal systems, so you'll find that many jurisdictions still have rules that do not mesh with tiny houses. As a result, even though building and parking a tiny house is fine in many areas (as we'll discuss in the next section), living in one is either expressly illegal or does not fall within any legal structure in the majority of locations. The most common sticking points and pitfalls include:

Minimum size

Some jurisdictions define the minimum square footage a house must have in order to be a legal place to live. Unfortunately that number is usually north of 500 square feet -- much larger than most tiny houses.

No flush toilet

Many building codes explicitly state that in order for a dwelling to be considered inhabitable, it must have at least one bathroom with a flush toilet.

However, tiny house builders opt to avoid the flush toilet. One reason is that finding a parking site that includes a septic system or sewer hookup is much harder than finding one that doesn't. Another is that putting in a septic system is a very expensive proposition, ranging from $5,000 to $20,000 depending on what work is needed.

Illegal loft bedroom

Many building codes do not allow ladder-accessed lofts due to fire safety concerns. That's a problem because lofts help tiny house dwellers get the maximum use out of a small footprint. For example, my tiny house's footprint is just 150 square feet, but thanks to my loft, I'm able to fit a comfy queen-sized bed.

Minimum room size

Though less common than other issues, some building codes define the minimum legal size for a bedroom. Since some entire tiny houses are less than 100 square feet, it's tough to meet minimum size requirements for specific rooms.

Not enough egress

Many building codes are designed to keep us safe, so it's no surprise that tiny houses do not meet many codes related to egress (a fancy word for "exit"). There's often a minimum window and door size to satisfy the requirements, and the small windows in your tiny house aren't big enough to count as legal forms of egress. On top of that, many codes require two forms of egress, so even if the tiny house has a full-size front door, it may be lacking a second acceptable exit route, particularly from any lofted areas.

Temporary structure for permanent living

This final problem is unique to tiny houses on wheels: Many building codes define a structure on wheels as a "temporary" structure and go on to specify a maximum length of time that one can inhabit such a structure. That means that depending on where a tiny house is parked, it may only be legal to live in it for a few months out of the year.

I know that was quite a list of potential pitfalls. I hope you're not feeling too discouraged! In reality, the zoning laws are enforced on a complaint-driven basis. My own house is subject to some or all of the issues above, and I have chosen to "fly under the radar" by parking my house in a mostly hidden location with the permission of the landowner. I've done what I can to minimize the chance of someone complaining, which (fingers crossed!) means my house and I are safe

While it is a pain in the butt, the more people who challenge the rules, the more aware jurisdictions will become of tiny houses, and progress will be made. In fact, there are actually some towns that have expressly legalized tiny houses. I'll tell you about them in Part 3: Further Reading and Resources.

Welcome to the tiny house movement. Now let's help you figure out how to navigate the ins and outs of tiny house parking!

Will a Tiny House be Legal in My Town?

By far the most common question I receive regarding tiny house parking is, "Will a tiny house be legal in My Town?" Unfortunately, there is no universal answer to that question, because the rules are different in every single town. The only thing true across the board is that there are very few places where it's completely legal to build, park, and live full time in a tiny house on wheels. Beyond that, you'll need to do your own research to find out what the rules are where you plan to live.

We've already discussed a few of the legal barriers tiny houses run into. Now let's break down some of the issues you're likely to encounter as you build, park, and live in your house and look at how you might be able to get around them.

Is it Legal to Build a Tiny House?

Jay Shafer, founder of The Tumbleweed Tiny House Company, built his house on a trailer. In his interview in the documentary *We the Tiny House People*, Jay explains that he did so to get around his town's building codes.

This workaround is possible in most places. When you build a structure (like a tiny house) on top of a trailer that is registered with a license plate, in the eyes of the law it's just load on a trailer, not a house. So building a tiny house on wheels is a way of skirting around the building laws that prevent many people from building tiny.

But what if you don't want to build your tiny house on a trailer? In that case, you have two options. Either you can work with your local building administrators from the start, or you can go "under the radar" and risk getting in trouble later on.

There's actually a third option, if you're willing to keep your house really small: the minimum square footage requirement. The exact number differs from town to town, but in many areas, only structures larger than a certain size -- often 120 square feet -- are subject to zoning codes. Depending on your area's requirements, you could legally build a stationary tiny house of up to 10 feet by 12 feet without getting any permits.

So far, then, we know that it's legal to build a tiny house on wheels in most places, and it's legal to build a tiny structure under a certain size in most places. Parking and living in that structure, though, are whole other matters entirely.

Is it Legal to Park a Tiny House?

If you're building your house on a foundation, you'll obviously need to choose its permanent location before you break ground. The fact that your tiny house will be on a traditional foundation makes finding a place to "park" it easier in some ways. For one, you'll do all your research up front, before you start building, meaning any legal hurdles should be cleared early on.

If your house is on wheels, on the other hand, you have the option of finding a temporary place to park it and moving it later if you run into problems. One good fallback is the ability to park your tiny house on wheels at an RV park or campground. Depending on the climate in your town, these facilities may be open all year round with amenities like power, water, and septic. Beware: You will pay more in rent for these parking spots and they will not be private.

Even if you do build your house on wheels to get around building regulations, it's likely that the town you plan to live in has some kind of regulations about parking temporary structures. These rules are often known as "setbacks," and they apply regardless of whether you're parking your house on someone else's land, or on an empty lot that you rent or own. Setbacks are designed to protect neighbors from having to deal with property owners turning their lawns into junk shows, and they do this by specifying where on the property certain things (houses, driveways, cars, etc.) can be placed in relation to the property lines.

Setbacks aren't usually a big deal since people who want to live in tiny houses in other people's yards often want privacy, and so opt to live in their backyards rather than out front.

In addition to setbacks, many jurisdictions require some kind of stable surface or "pad" on which to park your tiny house. The pad makes your house safer by providing a very stable and level place to park, but adds additional cost. This usually means pouring some kind of concrete foundation, or using gravel or crushed stone.

As I've mentioned above, *parking* the house isn't really a big problem legally. The real problem comes if you want to live in your tiny house full time and legally.

Is it Legal to Live In a Tiny House?

Even if you manage to build and park your tiny house without running up against the law, you're likely to get into trouble when it comes to actually living in it. If you try to get around permits and building codes to build your tiny house, you'll end up with something that is officially considered a temporary structure instead of a house. Remember that list of common sticking points that come with living in tiny houses from the previous section? This is when they start to kick in.

The pitfalls you face will depend on your jurisdiction's rules, but there are ways to identify and avoid them. Lots of tiny house dwellers have written about codes and tiny houses elsewhere. Rather than summarize their excellent articles here, I suggest you take a moment to read the originals:

Codes and Tiny Houses -- Laura Lavoie
In this article on Tiny House Listings, Laura Lavoie answers several of the most common questions when it comes to codes for living in a tiny house. tinyhouseparkingbook.com/codes

Where can you Park a Tiny House -- Macy Miller
In this article, Macy Miller talks about how tiny houses are viewed legally in different places, including an excellent explanation of how "Mobile Home" and "RV" are two different designations. tinyhouseparkingbook.com/park

Part 2:
Tiny House Parking How-To

Now that we know the lay of the land, we can get into the actual how-to of parking a tiny house. I'll start with some zoning basics to help you understand the lingo the laws are written with. I'll also tell you how to find the laws specific to where you live.. Next up, we'll talk about the different options for tiny house living (trailer, foundation, or hybrid) and how they will affect the legality of your tiny house. Then we'll move on to paying for your parking space, and finally, specific requirements of what features you'll need to best support you and your tiny house.

Zoning Basics

There's really no way around it: To figure out what's legal in your area, you're going to have to get your hands on a copy of your local zoning ordinance. But before we jump into how to do that and what to look for once you have it, there are a few basic zoning terms you'll need to know.

Zoning

In essence, zoning is the process that we've been talking about all along: the way that the government regulates what can be built where, how it can be built, and what you can do with it after it's been built. For a detailed definition, see tinyhouseparkingbook.com/zoning.

The best time to start researching zoning laws is before you frame a single wall or even buy your trailer. The zoning process is in many cases outdated, frustrating, and bureaucratic; even worse, the specific laws vary from town to town. What's okay where you currently live might be completely against the law five miles away. The more prepared you are going in to your build, the better off you'll be in the long run.

Many towns have moved their documents online, which means it's pretty easy to track down the zoning laws you'll need to abide by. I recommend beginning your tiny house journey with a simple Google search to find a copy of the local zoning ordinance. Searching for *"Your Town, Your Country zoning laws"* will likely turn up your town's website and a digital copy of the ordinance you're after.

Classification

Classification just means a certain category that comes with a set of rules. Though the specific classifications vary from town to town, a site's classification will determine what can be done with it. For example, in most places you can only have a retail storefront in a building and area that are classified as commercial.

Variance

A variance is when your town's zoning board recognizes that your project is against the rules, but decides to allow you to proceed with it anyway. If you're trying to build a tiny house with the permission of your local authorities, you will be likely be seeking a variance. See tinyhouseparkingbook.com/variance for a more detailed look at variances.

At the risk of repeating myself, the zoning process can and is different in every single town -- some towns may not consider a variance to be a big deal, while others may see it as a highly unusual request.

Temporary Structure

A temporary structure is one that won't be in the same place for more than a certain number of months. Temporary structures often include mobile trailers used at construction sites, small sheds and outbuildings, and so forth. They sometimes even include RVs and mobile homes, though many zoning ordinances define these structures separately (thus giving them their own set of rules).

Because these structures will be temporary, the rules governing how and where they can be put are often more lax. Unfortunately, there also tend to be limitations on how long you can live in them. It's possible your local zoning laws will view a tiny house on wheels as a temporary structure.

Finding Your Town's Zoning Bylaws

As I mentioned earlier, a simple Google search for *Your Town, Y(* *zoning laws* will likely yield the document you're looking for.

The document will almost certainly be in the PDF format. If you're on a Mac, you can open the PDF using the program Preview that came with your computer. On Windows, you'll need to download and install the free Adobe Reader from tinyhouseparkingbook.com/adobe.

The zoning ordinance will probably be pretty dense and boring. Luckily, you can use a few keywords to find the information you're after. Rather than manually look for these keywords, use the "find" feature in your PDF reader (CTRL + F on Windows or COMMAND + F on Mac) to search the document for the following words:

- temporary
- temporary structure
- mobile home
- camper
- manufactured home
- minimum size
- egress

Keep clicking the "next" button so you can find and read the sections of the document that are relevant to your tiny house. You may want to copy down any relevant sections for easy reference later.

Once you get a general idea of what your town's zoning laws are, you can decide if and how you want to approach your local zoning officials. You may decide that the laws are too unfriendly to tiny houses and opt to go under the radar. Or, you may choose to call your zoning office to get a read on how the people who work there feel about tiny houses and if they might be willing to work with you.

An entire book could be written about how to strategize for that process -- in fact, it has. Rather than go into detal here, I've collected several additional resources to help you with this process at tinyhouseparkingbook.com/resources.

Even if you have no idea what your town's zoning laws are, there's still plenty to talk about. However, it will be easier to choose the best path for you if you have some idea of what the laws are in your specific area.

Tiny House Types and the Law

The tiny house parking options available to you depend on the kind of tiny house you have. Your very first decisions regarding your tiny house -- whether to build it on wheels or on a foundation -- sets the stage for which legal battle you'll be fighting and which particular pitfalls you'll need to watch out for.

Trailer

As mentioned above, if you build your tiny house on a trailer, it probably won't be subject to building code, because it won't count as a building. The upside is that it gives you much more freedom when it comes to planning and designing your tiny house, but it creates a bit of a problem if you plan to live in it full time.

Your tiny house will likely only count as a "temporary structure," like an RV, and, although the regulations vary from state to state, you will probably find that you'll only be allowed to live (or "camp") in your tiny house for a month or so at a time. If you ignore these regulations, you'll technically be breaking the law.

The complications don't stop there. Depending on where you choose to park your tiny house, the rules may prevent you from hooking your house up to utilities, require you to park on a concrete slab or a particular distance away from other structures, and limit the choices available to you in terms of design.

If you decide to build your tiny house on a trailer, you'll need to find out what the rules are in your area and how they would apply to your house. If you comply with those regulations, you probably won't have any trouble. You will, however, probably end up moving a lot which, depending on your lifestyle, may be far from ideal.

You'll also want to research any rules that will apply if you want to move your tiny house within your state. Pay special attention to laws regarding height, width, and weight.

Your other option is to ignore the rules and hope that no one finds out. This is dangerous because it involves breaking the law, running the risk of losing your home, and potentially getting on the bad side of your neighbors.

Of course, living in a tiny house on wheels as a big list of benefits. First and foremost, it allows you to become a homeowner at the lowest possible cost-since you don't have to pay for land along with your house. And for people like me who aren't sure quite where they'll be living 5 years in the future, the ability to move your house with you rather than have to deal with selling it and buying a new property in a new location is invaluable.

To sum up, living in a tiny house on wheels is appealing because it offers the most personal freedom (from taxes and a permanent location). It also puts you in a legal grey area, which makes your living situation less certain but makes it easier for you to fly under the radar. Before you build or buy your tiny house, you'll need to decide whether or not you are comfortable with living on such shaky ground.

Foundation

The main alternative to living in a tiny house on wheels is to live in one that's built on a foundation, such as on a concrete slab or over a basement. This option also comes with pros and cons.

Building your tiny house on the ground rather than on a trailer means you'll also most likely need to purchase land, which will increase costs. Your home won't be mobile, so you'll be tied to one place. You'll also probably need to secure permission before you build and comply with the building codes and regulations in your area. As you know by now, the trouble with building codes is that the definition of a residential home (as opposed to a temporary structure) is usually too narrow to include tiny houses.

That said, building on a foundation certainly has its upsides. Without the limitations that come with building on a trailer, for instance, you'll have a lot more freedom when it comes to the shape and size of your tiny house. You can build it bigger, square, or with two full floors, if you want to.

Hybrid

There is a third option. It is possible to build tiny houses that's kept on a semi-permanent foundation but can be transported when necessary. The result is a house that's similar to a park-model mobile home.

The field of hybrid tiny houses is vast, and wading into it will just derail our parking discussion. If this option appeals to you, I'd encourage you to do some research on your own. As a starting point, the following article includes a more in-depth discussion of hybrid tiny houses, along with photos and examples of 13 such homes: tinyhouseparkingbook.com/notrailer

Besides the added flexibility this option provides, a hybrid tiny house comes with the benefit of being covered by current legislation. You can keep these houses anywhere that you can keep mobile homes. Remember that there are sometimes limits on how long you can live in a mobile home, so you'll need to look these up. You'll also need to find out and stick to the limits for objects that are transported as wide loads on trailers.

No matter which path you take -- trailer, foundation, or hybrid -- you're going to need to research the rules carefully in the town where you want to live to make sure your tiny house is as legal as possible.

Dealing with the Law

Regardless of the kind of tiny house you decide to live in, you have two choices in terms of how you deal with the legal side of living in a tiny house. You can choose to ask permission from local authorities and risk being told "no." We'll call this "asking permission first." Or you can choose to not ask permission and work to minimize the risk of getting caught. We'll call this "begging forgiveness later."

Ask Permission First

The more honest approach is to contact your local authorities to find out what the rules are in your municipality. If you can develop a positive relationship with the powers that be, you may be able to come to an arrangement that enables you to stay on the right side of the law and therefore avoid surprises later.

If you need to be one hundred percent certain that your tiny house will be completely legal when parked, this is really the only way to go. A tiny house on wheels can be moved to a new location if you run into trouble, but a tiny house on a foundation can't. Legality is especially true if you plan on living in your house full time. If the worst happens and you're told your stationery tiny house isn't fit for habitation, you'll be homeless.

The biggest risk with being fully legal from the start is that the authorities won't be open to the idea of tiny houses and will refuse to grant you permission to live in yours. You might go through the entire process and still get a "no." In that case, you may have to try another area or give up your tiny house, because going under the radar will be even harder and riskier at this point. Another risk is that asking permission may bring to light additional permits and general site requirements that will cost you more money. For example, you may be required to put in a septic system and or pour a concrete slab for your house. Rules vary so widely from town to town that you're not guaranteed to run into problems, but it's useful to know where the potential pitfalls lie.

There are certainly success stories. Laura Lavoie at 120squarefeet.com is one such example. She managed to get permission to live in her tiny house, built on a foundation in the Appalachian Mountains. She was able to talk to the right people and secure the necessary approvals to build "something" on her land. Because she lives in such a rural area, the rules weren't enforced as strictly as they might be in a city. In Laura's case, it made more sense to approach the authorities than to try to avoid them.

w Odom of tinyrevolution.us is another good example. Andrew
:d his tiny house to be completely legal. To satisfy the local powers
that be, he had to install it a particular way. That extra effort was worth it to
him. For more on the specifics of his build and an excellent primer on how
to approach the process of legalizing his tiny house, I highly recommend his
three-part series on the legal side of tiny house living at
tinyhouseparkingbook.com/legalseries.

Beg Forgiveness Later

The other option is to *not* ask permission and to then work to reduce your
risk of getting caught. If you can find somewhere relatively private to keep
your tiny house, you could opt to keep your living status to yourself and
hope that no one unfriendly to your cause notices and reports you to the
authorities.

Going under the radar is less risky if your tiny house is on wheels, since you
can just move to another parking spot if you run into trouble. However, if
you need to stay in one place (for your job, maybe) or you want to build
your tiny house on a foundation, this option may be too uncertain for you.
As I've mentioned, you might face fines if someone alerts the authorities to
your illegal house. You could even be forced to move out of the house you
invested tens of thousands of dollars in.

That's exactly what happened to Jonathan Bellows from Southeast
Michigan (tinyhouseparkingbook.com/jonathan1). After building his house,
Jonathan found out that his county considered dwellings under 960 square
feet to be uninhabitable, and no township or city within 100 miles of his
home would allow his tiny house. Jonathan spoke to code and zoning
officials and attended town hall meetings to plead his case, but eventually
he realized it was no good.

Not one to give up, he bought some land anyway and parked his tiny house
in the trees, so that it couldn't be seen from the road. But his unfriendly
neighbor could see his tiny house and, just a few months after he moved in,
Jonathan found a notice on his door, identifying his tiny house as a camper
and saying he was in violation of the law. The zoning authorities said they

would take legal action if Jonathan didn't comply with the laws. Since he had no way to add the necessary square footage to his tiny house on wheels, and didn't want to fight the decision, he was forced to move out.

Ultimately, Jonathan decided it wasn't worth trying to hide his house again in Michigan. He has since moved to Oregon and turned the experience into a positive one, but his story demonstrates the risk that comes with attempting to live illegally under the radar.

Not everyone feels the way Jonathan does, though. You may decide you're willing to risk it, just as Erin did (tinyhouseparkingbook.com/erin). She knew that living in a tiny house meant living on shaky ground, so she decided to let go of the idea of permanence. Whereas others might worry that they'd be heartbroken if they were forced to leave their homes, Erin says that, "moving a house is not heartbreaking. I've been through some heartbreak, everybody has, and it's never something so silly as moving."

If you're thinking begging permission might be your preferred approach, there are certainly ways you can minimize your chances of getting into trouble with the law. Here are a few ideas:

Find a Location Where Your House is Not Visible from the Road

The key to avoiding contact with local zoning officials is reducing your visibility. If your house isn't visible from the road, fewer people will know it exists. That lowers the number of people who could potentially object to your tiny house and reduces the chance someone will complain about it.

Find a Location Where Your House is Not Visible to Neighbors

Believe it or not, your neighbors are an even greater concern than the general public. Here's why: In most places in the US, enforcing zoning laws isn't like enforcing drug or crime laws. There are no zoning police walking the streets, looking for violations. Rather, zoning violations are brought to light through a complaints-based process. Residents can call the zoning board if they notice their neighbor building something that looks illegal or annoys them, and put a stop to the build that way.

If you can be hidden from as many neighbors as possible, you'll greatly reduce (or even eliminate) the risk of one of them complaining about you and your house.

Be Proactive about Talking to Potential Snitches

In practice, it's very unlikely that you'll be able to hide your tiny house completely from view. The next best course of action is to be proactive by talking to your immediate neighbors before moving in or building your house there. That way, you can find out if they have any concerns.

Later in this book, you'll read an in-depth interview with Alek Lisefski, who used this strategy to keep his house under the radar. Alek spoke to his neighbors to address any concerns they had, and that one of them requested the house not obscure a nice view he had. By finding that out in advance, Alek was able to avoid potential conflict. He's been living in his house without any issues for close to two years as I write this.

So, is begging permission the right route for you? Ask yourself if you're comfortable breaking the law, potentially evade paying taxes, and maybe even losing money. If the answer is no, then flying under the radar with your tiny house probably isn't for you.

One final note: At the time of writing, it's much more common for people to build and live in tiny houses on wheels *without* the owners asking for permission. After all, as the old saying goes: It's easier to beg forgiveness than ask permission. That doesn't mean it's necessarily better, though. Which approach is right for you will depend on your personal preferences and situation.

Paying for Your Land

Whether you go under the radar or toe the line, there are a few ways you can secure land to live on. You could rent, buy, trade, or, if you're really lucky, live for free on a family member's land. Each of these three variations comes with its own set of problems and advantages.

Rent

If you don't have the money to buy land, or you don't want to make that kind of commitment, you may be able to find someone who's willing to let you rent theirs and grant you access to their utilities. You could rent someone's back yard or driveway, an empty plot of land, a field, a campsite, or any other piece of land that's not being used.

This can be a very affordable option, as tiny houses don't tend to need much more than the few hundred square feet or so that they sit on. Chris and Malissa Tack (chrisandmalissa.com) pay $300 per month. Macy Miller (minimotives.com) pays $200.

The main downside to renting is that you don't have control over your land. You could be asked to leave at any point, and you may not be able to adapt the land to suit your needs. For example, your landlord might not be happy for you to create a garden or drain your grey water. Rental opportunities can also be hard to come by.

If you're interested in renting land for your tiny house, Craigslist and even your local paper's classifieds are a good place to start. Later on in the book, I'll share many more specialized resources for finding land to rent.

Buy

If you have the money and are willing to commit to one location, buying your own land might be a good option for you. Doing so gives you complete control over your home, and you can stay there indefinitely -- provided you've cleared your tiny house with the proper authorities ahead of time, that is.

And that's the main risk that comes with purchasing land for your tiny house: running into trouble with the authorities. The more permission you can get before you buy the land, the less likely you are to run into trouble. However, you could end up having to leave your home and sell the land, like Jonathan did. Buying property can be enough of a bureaucratic nightmare without the whole process being for nothing.

Another downside for some people is that this option can be quite restrictive, both geographically and financially. Land is very expensive, and if you invest in it, you'll probably have to commit to staying on it for at least a year or two for your investment to pay off.

If your sticking point is financial, there are ways to offset the cost of buying land. You could buy a house with a yard, park your tiny house in it, and rent out the house. This way, other people pay the mortgage and you can live for free on your own property. Of course, becoming a landlord means taking on a lot of responsibilities, but if you can afford to buy, this option is worth considering.

If you think buying land is for you, Laura Lavoie recommends working with a realtor to find affordable and suitable land. It is unlikely that you will be able to find land to buy in a town or city, so you may have to be willing to live in the countryside to go this route.

Trade

Instead of buying or renting, or in addition to renting, you could trade work or goods for land and utilities. Whether you're a skilled professional or not, there's bound to be a way that you could compensate a landowner for letting you live on their land.

One option is to offer your professional skills. You could teach, coach, consult, mentor, or provide any other services to your host for free. If none of your professional skills were of interest, you could offer to do odd jobs around the house. For example, you could mow the lawn, clean, fix anything that breaks, do the owners' shopping, or provide childcare. You might also be interested in looking for caretaking opportunities; you may be able to live cheaply on someone's land in exchange for keeping an eye on an empty property. There are even organizations dedicated to helping people with special needs find others to share their houses or land with in exchange for the help they need on a day to day basis. See homeshare.org/ for more info. Finally, you could trade goods, such as vegetables you grow or your art.

Before you proceed with a trade situation, there's one caveat. A lawyer friend once told me that a verbal agreement isn't worth the paper it's written on. If you do work out a trade scenario, get some kind of written agreement in advance so that you don't run into problems down the road.

Live for Free

This final option won't be available to many people, but if it's open to you, it's worth considering. If you're lucky enough to know someone who has land they don't use or belong to a family that owns land, you may be able to live on it rent-free.

This situation may sound ideal, but be careful! There are certainly issues that can pop up unexpectedly. You may feel beholden to the owners to do favors or otherwise put yourself out because there's a feeling that you "owe" your landlord something. Family dynamics can come into play, and in the event of a disagreement, you're at the mercy of the owners' whims if there's no official agreement or terms in place. To avoid future conflict, make sure both you and the landowner know exactly what you're agreeing to. Draw up a contract or agreement both parties are happy with before you move in.

As appealing as living for free on family land might be, it's not without caveats. Proceed with caution and it could be a great setup for your tiny house.

Now that we've looked at how to pay for your tiny house land, we can move on to the nitty gritty! Namely, what you'll need to look for in any potential parking place for your tiny house that will make your life there comfortable (or even possible in the first place).

Requirements & What to Look for

Once you have an idea of how you'll pay for your land, you'll want to make sure any land you consider meets with your requirements. That means you'll need to know what those requirements are. While most of the features and characteristics you look for will be nice-to-haves, there are some features that you won't be able to go without. As always, exactly what these requirements are will depend on you, your tiny house, and your lifestyle. The following list of common requirements is a good starting point for determining what you'll want your land to have.

Level, Stable Ground

If you've ever tried to park an RV or mobile home, you know that it's important to park it on a flat piece of land. The same goes for your tiny house.

An ideal piece of land will already be level and ready for you to park your house on. If you're purchasing land, you might be able to flatten out a slope or hill, but make sure doing so is possible before you buy! Talk to an excavator to find out what your options are. If you're renting, you may still be able to alter the landscape to accommodate your tiny house. However, you'll need to get permission from the landowner before making changes, and you'll probably need to cover the costs. As with buying, make sure you find out what you can and can't do before agreeing to anything.

Let's face it: A level stretch of ground isn't the only geographical feature you'll want a suitable piece of land to have. You can't park your tiny house on a swamp any more than you can park it on the side of a steep hill. Well, you could, but it probably wouldn't stay there for very long! Make sure any land you buy or rent will be able to hold your tiny house. Very soft ground as well as poorly drained areas that are prone to flooding or wetness will prove challenging. The same goes for swamp and marshland, wetlands, floodplains, and so on. Don't forget that land that may look great when you view it on a hot, dry summer's day could be completely squishy for two months each spring.

Hookups

Many tiny house dwellers choose to live on-grid, meaning they're connected to public utilities such as electricity, water, and drainage. If you want to live on-grid, you'll need to choose land that comes with the proper hookups for these utilities. If you choose to park your tiny house in someone's backyard, you should just be able to connect your tiny house up to the main house. If you park at a campsite, the hookups provided for RVs should work just fine.

If, however, you decide to park on an empty piece of land, you may want to find one that either used to have a building on it or is ready for a building to be built on it. Completely empty pieces of land in the countryside may have no hookups whatsoever, and and putting the necessary ones in often requires extra time, planning permission, and more money than you may want to spend. If you go this route, do plenty of research ahead of time so that you know what you're getting yourself into before you buy the land!

It's not enough, though, to just make sure the hookups are there. Whether you're buying or renting land, check that the utilities you're planning to use are compatible with your tiny house. Does your water system need an external source, like a hose? Make sure the property has one. Will the voltage of the existing electrical hookup work with your system? If not, it won't do you much good. If you plan to live in someone's yard, make sure they're okay with the idea of you setting up a composting bin for your waste (if you install a composting toilet as I recommend in *Tiny House Decisions*).

It's not a dealbreaker if the hookups aren't ready or available at your site. You'll just need to know in advance and plan to work around them. For example, if you can't get electricity at your site, you'll need to plan for solar power or a generator.

Of course, it may be that you're planning to live completely off-grid and would relish the opportunity to live independently in the middle of nowhere. In that case, go ahead! But if you'd rather not accidentally become the next star of *Cast Away*, make sure you find out exactly what any piece of land you consider buying does and does not have in the way of hookups.

Internet

Do you need to be able to connect to the internet from your tiny house? Well then, make sure there's a way to do it on any land you consider using. Given the fact that I'm writing this chapter using Google Drive, an internet-based word processor, you can probably guess that having internet access is crucial to me!

If you're parked behind someone's house or in a residential area, you shouldn't have trouble piggybacking onto a neighbor's wi-fi (with permission, of course). But if you're following your dreams of becoming a mountain-side tiny house hermit, the coverage may not be there. Either way, do your research beforehand.

Waste Removal Systems

Whether you plan to live on- or off-grid, you'll need to find a way to safely dispose of your water waste. That includes everything from sewage to shower runoff.

Who doesn't love a flush toilet? Well, many tiny house dwellers choose to avoid them, because a flush toilet requires land that comes with a way to dispose of black water, the sewage water from your toilet. This might mean a hookup to a sewer system, a septic system, or a black water storage tank (that you'll need to empty...gross!).

I've got really good news for you: You can skip having to deal with sewage altogether by installing a composting toilet in your tiny house. I'm a big fan of the humanure-style toilet because it can be built for under $100 in materials and is safe and easy to use. However, depending on your level of commitment to compost, there are commercial composting toilets that do more of the work for you. For more on this topic, check out *The Humanure Handbook* by Joseph Jenkins (you'll find a link to it at tinyhouseparkingbook.com/resources). But I digress.

You'll also need a way to drain grey water, the non-sewage wastewater from sinks, showers, and washing machines -- in other words, any wastewater that hasn't come into contact with feces. It might contain soap, hair, dirt, food, lint, bacteria, grease, and cleaning products.

Dumping grey water into the nearby pond isn't a good idea because it has the potential to pollute the environment and harm wildlife. But there are plenty of easy ways to dispose of this kind of water safely, whether you're living on rented land or your own land. Before constructing any kind of grey water disposal system, check with your local authorities in case they have any regulations. (I don't have to tell you by now how much they love their regulations.)

Provided the powers that be don't have any objections, a popular way to get rid of grey water is to redirect it into a garden, where it can water some plants or trees. In a perfect world, your site would come with a flat area to park your house on, some plants or trees to drink up the grey water, and a downhill slope between the two so that gravity could do all the work.

Does that mean you should rule out a piece of land just because it doesn't have the perfect house-to-slope-to-garden setup? Of course not. There are many ways to create a grey water disposal system, and, as long as you're legally allowed to dispose of your own grey water in your area, you should be able to find a way to do so once the land is yours. Don't base your tiny house parking decisions on grey water alone, but bear it in mind when considering land.

To find out more about disposing of grey water safely when living in a tiny house, read *An Introduction to Grey Water in Your Tiny House* at tinyhouseparkingbook.com/greywater.

Price

Unless you're independently wealthy, price will probably play a big role in determining where you can and can't park your tiny house. Renting a piece of land can be very affordable. As we've discussed, many tiny house dwellers pay only a few hundred dollars a month to park their houses on someone else's land. Some also trade their services in exchange for the land they live on.

When it comes to buying land, prices will vary enormously depending on country, state, city versus countryside, the quality of the land, and so on. You will likely find that land is significantly cheaper in remote parts of the word, where there are no hookups, shops, or even other people (this is either your biggest dream or worst nightmare!).

Here's where knowing what you're looking for before you start hunting for land comes in handy: You won't snap up a great bargain, only to realize after you've signed on the dotted line that your new property is lacking in basic necessities. Have a price range in mind and work with a real estate agent to find the best deal for you.

Work out your budget carefully, making sure to take into account any extra or hidden charges. Find out what additional fees there will be and account for them in your budget. Make sure you know exactly how you will pay off any loans or repayments before you sign on the dotted line.

When you find somewhere you'd like to park your tiny house, remember that you don't have to pay the asking price. You are well within your rights to negotiate and haggle. Again, consult with an expert on what prices to offer, and don't be offensive with your offers, but do try to get the best possible price. The same goes for agreeing on a rental price.

Proximity

Do you want to live ten miles from civilization, or are you the kind of person who likes to be in the thick of things? Do you need to be able to get into downtown within a matter of minutes, or do you like the peace and quiet that comes with being surrounded by nature?

Of all the considerations we've discussed so far, proximity may be the one that depends most on individual preference. Only you can decide what's right for you. Work out how near or far any land you consider is from the places you visit regularly. Find out where the stores, post office, cafes, restaurants, bars, religious buildings, train and bus stations, and schools are. Ask yourself where you need to go on a regular basis, how you would get there, and how long it would take. Then keep that information in mind as you look at land options.

Climate

The climate and temperature of where you live will have a bigger impact on your tiny house design than you might think. The temperature range will guide your heating and air conditioning choices. The available sunlight will determine whether or not solar power will be a viable option for you.

If you already have a tiny house, you'll have to either choose the place you live based on the features you tiny house has or be willing to change them. If your tiny house is still in the works, you can plan ahead to make sure your house is compatible with the climate in which you want to live. Either way, take the time to consider how the climate of a particular region will affect your tiny house before you commit to land that's located there.

Size

If your house is like most tiny houses, coming in between 100 and 300 square feet, you technically don't need much land to park it on. You could easily fit into many people's backyards.

That said, you might want more space than that. Many tiny house owners like to create gardens around their homes. Some grow vegetables. Some create beautiful landscapes. Some build fire pits. You might want or need to create your own composting area or store your bike or car. And if you have pets or kids, you'll probably want plenty of space for them to run around in.

On the other hand, while owning several acres of land in the countryside might sound like a dream, it comes with a fair amount of responsibility. Are you prepared to cut that much grass on a regular basis? Will you actually use all that space?

Work out how much land you would like before you start your search. That way, you'll be less likely to get distracted by offers that aren't quite right for you.

People and Neighborhood

Neighbors can make or break a home. If your tiny house is built on wheels, you can at least move if you lock horns with your neighbors, but let's face it: moving is a pain in the butt! Save yourself some hassle by checking out your neighbors before you commit to living somewhere.

Regardless of whether you're buying or renting land, find out who lives on either side of or around you. If you're hoping to live in the countryside, get to know any locals by visiting the nearest post office, shop, or bar. Chat with the people there to get a sense of what they're like. Use your charms! Try to talk with anyone you're likely to interact with on a regular basis and find out their attitudes towards tiny houses. This is particularly important if you're planning to live under the radar. You don't want your neighbor reporting you to the authorities.

While you're at it, also find out if there's anything unusual about either the land or the area you're hoping to move to. Is there a festival that turns the remote village into a party town once a year? Is there an innocent-looking stream that floods the valley every spring? Ask around to make sure you know exactly what you're getting yourself into.

If you'll be renting, you have an extra category of people to scope out: the landowners. Now it's time to use the skills you learned in kindergarten and make friends!

If you don't already know the landowners, get to know them. Find out their thoughts on tiny house living. Ask them about their routines and daily lives. Interview them if necessary. Moving onto someone's land is a big deal, so don't rush into it.

If you already know the landowners, you may think you're off the hook. However, turning friendships into business and landlord-tenant relationships can change the dynamics of a relationship, so make sure you'll be able to deal with any weirdness that might arise. Ask yourself if you'd feel comfortable seeing them regularly, going to them with any concerns or problems that might crop up, and even paying them.

Notice Period

This final consideration only applies to you if you're planning to rent: Find out how much notice you'll have to give before leaving the property. I'd recommend having a nice heart-to-heart with your landlord to talk about what would happen if, for example, a neighbor complained and you had to move quickly. Too short a period may leave you scrambling to make alternate arrangements, but the opposite may mean you're stuck living on the property for longer than you'd like should something go wrong.

Whew! I'm glad we got through that together. I know there's a lot to keep track of when you're looking for land for your tiny house, but hopefully you have a good list of questions to ask and issues to look out for.

General Strategies for Finding Land

Now that you have a sense of what your land options are and what to look for when considering a spot for your tiny house, how do you actually go about finding land to look at? Here are a few strategies you can use to find land for your tiny house.

Reach Out to Friends and Family

The easiest place to start your search is with friends and family. If you know someone who has some land, whether that's an entire field or just a spare corner in a garden, you might be able to arrange to park your tiny house there. Whether you rent the land or live there for free, just keep in mind what I've said about how business can change relationship dynamics, and get the agreement in writing.

Even if your friends and family don't own any suitable land themselves, they may be able to help. Do they know someone who could hook you up with some land? At the very least, they could spread the word and keep an ear out for you. Ask them to put their feelers out and let you know if they come across any opportunities. Since you've already generated a list of must-have features for yourself after reading the last section, pass it along to the people helping you out. That way any offers you do get will be better tailored to what you're after.

Get Involved in the Tiny House Community

Another great place to start is within the tiny house community itself. If you have friends who live in tiny houses, make sure they know you're in the market for a place to park your tiny house, as they're likely to be more clued in to what you're looking for than your non-tiny-house friends and family.

What if you don't currently know anyone in the tiny house community? Now might be the time to get involved. Here are a few ways you can get to know some tiny house folk.

Join Facebook Groups

Social media is probably the easiest way to find out about tiny house opportunities. Tiny house Facebook groups in particular are full of useful information and people eager to help. Here are some of the most active tiny house Facebook groups to get you started:

- Tiny House Community - facebook.com/TinyHouseCommunity
- Tiny Yellow House - tinyhouseparkingbook.com/tinyyellowhouse
- Tiny House Listings - facebook.com/tinyhouselistings
- Tiny House Hub - facebook.com/TinyHouseHub
- Tiny House Design - facebook.com/tinyhousedesign
- Tiny House Events - facebook.com/tinyhouseevents
- Building the Tiny House - facebook.com/buildingthetinyhouse

You might also want to join Facebook groups for your local area. Some towns and cities even have groups specifically for buying and selling. Post your request for land in these groups...who knows who might see it!

Use *Meetup.com*

Meetup.com is an online portal designed to help people meet others with similar interests in their area. There are two ways to use this site to meet fellow tiny house enthusiasts: look for an existing tiny house group or start your own.

Once you've joined or created a group, start attending or hosting regular in-person events. Perhaps you could even put on a networking event to bring together tiny house enthusiasts and local building contractors. By connecting with other tiny house dwellers and hopefuls, you'll expand your network of tiny-house-friendly people and therefore make it that much easier to find land for your house.

Go to Workshops

Tiny house manufacturers and enthusiasts regularly hold tiny house building workshops in many parts of the US. It goes without saying that anyone who attends one of these workshops is interested in the tiny house movement, so if you can find one in your state, this could be a great way to make connections in your area. Just search for tiny house workshops on Google or visit the websites of nearby tiny house manufacturers to find out what's being offered in your area.

As well as talking to the other participants, ask the workshop leaders if they know of any land you might be able to live on. They may also have tips for finding a good site somewhere in your region.

An upside of this approach is that in addition to possibly finding land, you'll also learn valuable tiny house planning and construction skills. The potential downsides are that workshops can be quite expensive and are usually only held in more major metropolitan areas.

Go to Events

Occasionally there are tiny house events, such as the *Tiny House Conference*, which draw members of the community from far and wide (tinyhouseconference.com). These events provide great opportunities to talk to tiny house experts, manufacturers, and builders who might be able to give you some pointers.

Advertise

Another approach you can take to find land is to advertise. There are lots of people who have lots of land that they don't even know what to do with -- they just need to find you! By spreading the word far and wide, you'll increase the chance of making that connection.

Here are a few advertising methods you might want to try.

Use Classifieds and Craigslist

Create a classifieds or Craigslist.org post to introduce yourself, outline what you're looking for and what tiny houses are, and explain what you'd be willing to pay or trade for land. If possible, include some photos of your tiny house so people can see how charming it is. Be careful, of course, when using these kinds of anonymous, online services.

Distribute Posters

Ask shop owners, churches, community centers, and libraries if you can put up "wanted" posters about your tiny house. You could also display posters in your car or, depending on where it's parked, on your tiny house itself. Include similar information as above: what you're looking for, a photo of your house, and some contact info.

Social Media

Use social networks such as Facebook, Twitter, and YouTube to spread the word. The best part about social media is that you can ask your friends and family to share your message for you to amplify your search. Who knows? Maybe your search will go viral!

Join Nextdoor

Nextdoor.com is a private social network site for neighborhoods. By joining it, you can connect with the people who live nearby and perhaps reach out to see if anyone knows of land you could live on.

Follow the Right Websites

Reading blogs and websites is an easy way to stay in the loop and to hear about any opportunities that come up. Here are a handful of the most useful websites when it comes to finding land for your tiny house.

Tiny House Websites

TinyHouseCommunity.com is an online hub that provides useful information to help connect tiny house owners with builders, communities, and each other. It includes maps of tiny house communities and builders, a classifieds section, and an events calendar, so it's a perfect resource if you're looking for somewhere to park your tiny house.

TinyHouseMap.com is an interactive map that you can use to search for tiny house builders, tiny houses for sale or rent, events, workshops, people, and open house opportunities.

TinyHouseParking.com (not associated with this book) also provides an interactive map, which can be configured to display parking places available for rent or purchase. You can even create a "tiny house parking wanted" ad here.

Landowner Websites

Be prepared to step outside of the tiny house community in your hunt for land. You may have better luck finding land for sale or rent on websites and through organizations for landowners and seekers than you are on a site for the tiny house community.

Sites such as *LandWatch.com*, *LandsofAmerica.com*, and *LandAndFarm.com* are great places to start. Run searches according to your requirements on as many websites advertising land for rent or sale as possible.

Forums

You may be able to find some leads in online tiny house forums such as *SmallHouseForum.com* and *The Tiny House Forums* (livingbiginatinyhouse.com/tiny-house-forums/). Check out forums in the landowner, self-build, and sustainability communities, such as *Selfbuild.com*, as well.

Set Your Search Up for Success

Finding land for your tiny house doesn't have to be a daunting task. To make sure you're putting out the clearest and most appealing message, here are some final tips:

Know Your Audience

Before you approach someone, consider what's in it for them. What do you have that your prospective landlord might want?

Of course, the answer will depend on the kinds of people you approach. If your prospective landlord lives in a really wealthy area, gaining a few hundred extra dollars a month might not make hosting you worth it for them. But receiving one-of-a-kind custom-made jewelry or pottery (if you happen to be an artist) just might.

Keep in mind that certain people may be more likely to accept your offer than others, so it's worth giving some thought to who you approach. Senior citizens, for example, may have more space than families and need a bit of help around the house. Farmers are also likely to have plenty of land and probably won't say no to an extra hand around the farm. People already familiar with the tiny house movement might also be more amenable to the idea of hosting a tiny house than those who've never heard of it.

Be Patient

Bear in mind that a lot of people will not have heard of tiny houses before. The concept of tiny living might confuse them, so be patient and have lots of photos on hand. Explain your reasons for wanting to live in a tiny house, and be as friendly and polite as possible.

Make a Good Impression

Make sure your tiny house looks nice and is well maintained. The same applies to you. Strangers will be much more likely to consider welcoming you into their home if you look like you'll take care of it, so make sure you scrub up well. Tidy your tiny house, give it a fresh lick of paint, and do your hair!

Think Outside the Box

Be creative. Tiny houses are still a novelty, so just giving people the opportunity to see and interact with one is a great way to get people interested. Here are a couple of ideas to get you started.

Create a video of yourself and your tiny house. Explain who you are, what your background is, and why you want to live in a tiny house. Film a virtual tour of your home. Explain how everything works, focusing on any special requirements you might have (like how you'd connect your utilities).

Host a "get to know you" get-together at your tiny house. Invite people over to see firsthand what tiny living looks like. Let them poke around and ask questions to satisfy their curiosity.

Even though the search for land can seem overwhelming, there are tons of resources out there, and with some time and energy, I am sure you'll be able to find a spot that suits you and your tiny house!

Where to Park Your Your Tiny House While You're Building It

Our next topic is really only applicable if you're building rather than buying your tiny house on wheels: finding a good place to build your house.

It's not essential that you find the future home of your tiny house before you build it. If you're comfortable living in a house that's in a legal grey area, you may also be comfortable investing time and money into building a house you don't yet have land for. As Aldo says, there's always another campsite (goldthreadtinyhouse.blogspot.com).

But, whether you've got everything planned or you're just hoping it all works out, one thing you do need to secure as soon as possible is the land you're going to build your tiny house on. There are a number of options and considerations to bear in mind when it comes to choosing this space.

Options

The options available to you will largely depend on who you know and how much money you have to spend.

If you know someone who owns land, or if you're buying the land on which you will eventually live, you could of course build your tiny house on that. This is likely to be cheaper than renting a separate space. Just must make sure the land has everything you'll need (this next section will help you determine those needs) before you go this route.

Sometimes, though, that option isn't ideal or even possible. Maybe you haven't found land yet, or maybe it's too far away from the nearest town (where you'll get supplies, services, and help) to be convenient while you're building. I built my house in my parents' yard, which was much closer to town than the land where I'd eventually park. I never ceased to be amazed by how often I needed to run to the hardware store to get something I was missing and was grateful that it was only a 10-minute drive from my building site. Using someone else's space can also come with its own perks, like access to tools or expertise while you're working.

If, for whatever reason, your house's final destination isn't ideal for building, start by spreading the word that you're looking for some land. Large warehouses, storage facilities, and barns are particularly ideal places to build tiny houses. Contact any businesses, farms, and ranches in your area that might have enough space to store a tiny house. You may be able to rent or trade work for a section of their building or land.

This approach worked well for Andrea Tremols and Cedric Baele (charlestontinyhouse.blogspot.co.uk). They worked for the non-profit *Sustainable Warehouse* for free, deconstructing old homes in exchange for free lumber and the use of the non-profit's huge storage warehouse.

Considerations

To find a great place to build your tiny house, it's not enough to just take any old spot you find. There are some additional considerations you'll want to keep in mind to make sure the space you settle on is a good fit for you and your tiny house

Time Frame

When considering your options for parking what will become your tiny house, bear in mind your timescale for building the house. That includes both how long you expect the building process will take and any breaks you'll need along the way.

I wish I could tell you exactly how long it will take you to build your tiny house, but the answer is different for everyone. The amount of time it takes will depend on how much time you have available to work on the house, your skills and experience, and whether or not you'll be getting help from friends or contractors.

What I can do is give you a couple of real-world examples. Gabriella and Andrew could have moved into their tiny house after putting in 117.5 hours of work. That's hardly a month of full-time work. However, not only is Andrew a professional builder, their tiny house wasn't actually complete at this point. Then there's me: I thought my house would only take three months to build…and it took thirteen, working mostly part time with one hired (professional) helper!

If you can work full time on building your tiny house and you're a super pro builder, you may be able to complete the project in as little as two months. If your building skills are closer to average, it will probably take closer to twelve. If you have a full-time job and can only work on your house part time, the construction will likely take one to three years. Whatever your situation, it's always better to overestimate how much time it will take then underestimate!

Of course, there are plenty of ways to shorten this timeframe. You could figure out how to put in more of your own time. You could also hire someone to do the work for or with you. Another option, if you're sure you want to build some of the house yourself but you have limited time or funds, is to buy the shell or beginnings of a tiny house and complete it yourself.

The point of all this talk of time frames is this: When choosing a space in which to build your tiny house, make sure it will be available for the entire time that you need it. If you can't guarantee this, at least make sure your tiny house will be in a portable condition (framing and sheathing completed) by the time you need to move it.

What about breaks? You might not be planning to take any breaks, but if nothing else, climate will both have an impact on when you can and cannot build.

If you live in an area where winters are cold, snowy, and difficult, start building as early in the year as possible. You won't be guaranteed to finish in time, but you should aim to get as far into the build as you can before the weather turns. I live in Vermont, where working outside becomes difficult in October and nearly impossible in December. That meant I needed to have the exterior of my tiny house built and waterproofed by November, when the first snowfall came. I began in June and only just finished in time.

The same goes for difficult summers. If you live in a climate where it's not possible to work outside all day, every day in the summer, factor time out into your planning or find an indoor construction site with air conditioning!

Size

Measure the area you're considering using to ensure that it's big enough to hold your completed tiny house. This isn't the time to guess! Get out your designs and measure the space properly.

You don't just need space for your house, though. You'll also need to work around it, carry bulky objects, and maneuver long planks of wood. While you're measuring the space, make sure there will be enough room around your tiny house for you to work in as well as use any tools or supplies you're going to need.

Finally, check that you'll be able to get your completed tiny house, tools, truck, and furniture both into and out of the space. Make sure all the necessary doors and openings are usable before you agree to anything. I can't imagine anything worse than building your dream home only to realize it's stuck inside a random warehouse!

Shelter

Depending on where you live, you may or may not need your tiny house to be covered as you build it. Does yours need shelter? Here are two points to consider when making that decision.

First, you need to make sure your house is protected from the elements. This doesn't necessarily mean you have to build it inside, but you definitely have to work out how to protect your building project from getting too wet or being damaged by wind. For me, this meant rigging up a tarp system to protect my subfloor and framing from rain before the roof was on. You can see a photo of what that looked like at tinyhouseparkingbook.com/sheathing.

Second, plan ahead for the weather conditions in your area. It's a lot easier to work on your house while it's raining, for instance, if you're inside! In

Vermont where it gets very cold, I worked hard to get the exterior of the house done by November so that I could move on to the interior work during the winter.

Storage

Your house isn't the only thing you'll want to protect from the weather as you build. You'll also want to be able to keep your tools indoors, or at least well covered and protected from the elements and thieves. Ideally, your chosen building site will have a lockable space that you can keep them in.

I can tell you from experience that building a tiny house is a lot more enjoyable when you don't have to haul heavy tools around all day. Chop saws and table saws are pretty heavy! It's worth trying to find a safe way to store any tools you'll use as close as possible to your tiny house.

Cost

It's no good finding the perfect building location if you can't afford it. You don't want to run out of money partway through your build, so factor this space into your budget before you start building, and don't let yourself be tempted by a great space that's beyond your means!

Facilities

Finally, work out which facilities you'll need. Perhaps most importantly, you'll need somewhere to relieve yourself. Even more importantly, how are you going to plug in your power tools? Access to reliable electricity is a must. You might also need or want access to water, a kettle, a fridge, somewhere to sit down, and so on.

For the most part, this will be a case of personal preference, so make sure you figure out what your requirements are before you sign for a place. You don't want to have to move your tiny house in progress just because you can't go a whole day without a cup of coffee!

Now that you are more tuned in to the requirements you may have for a building site, we can move on to the fun stuff: Living happily ever after in your tiny house!

Living Happily Ever After

At this point, you're getting to be quite the tiny house parking expert. You may think you've learned all you need to know, but not so fast! Even after you're all done building your house, you'll need to actually get it to the land that you've chosen (assuming the house is on wheels). And once you get there, there are still a few details left to handle.

Moving Your Tiny House

If your tiny house is on wheels, once it's built and ready to be parked in its new home, you'll have to deal with the scary time that is moving day! Prepare yourself for a nail-biting few moments when your tiny house first starts to move, particularly if you've built it yourself. Waiting to see whether or not it moves without collapsing in a heap is pretty nerve-wracking. And once you realize that's not going to happen, seeing your house rolling down the road is exciting!

Of course, there are other times when you might need or want to move your tiny house too. You might get a job in a new region. You might want to go on a tour of the country. You might end your rental agreement or buy your own land. Or, sadly, you might be asked to move your tiny house if you've been caught living in it illegally.

Whatever the reason, there are a few things you should know about moving your tiny house.

Preparing to Move Your Tiny House

Your house may be on wheels, but you can't just up and move it whenever you feel like it. You'll need to plan ahead and make sure everything is in place for the move.

Perhaps the most important thing to do is to ensure that your tiny house is roadworthy. This includes making sure your trailer is registered and insured (with both comprehensive and collision coverage), displaying a valid license plate, verifying that your house meets the road requirements, obtaining a permit if necessary, checking that everything (such as tail lights and turn signals) is working as it should, and ensuring that the vehicle towing your house is street legal and insured.

You shouldn't need a special permit to move your tiny house, unless it doesn't meet the road requirements. These differ widely, so look them up for every state or country you'll be passing through. In the US, a general guideline is that vehicles should not be taller than 13'6" or wider than 8'6". As well as size, you'll need to take into account the gross vehicle weight, which is the combined weight of the trailer, the house, and any items inside the house.

Just as with any move, you'll need to pack your belongings. Some of your possessions may be able to travel in the house, but many will need to be packed into boxes and transported separately so that nothing breaks in transit. Anything that you do keep in your house should be secured so it doesn't fall and roll around inside the house while it's on the road.

Choosing a Truck

Unless you've managed to build a self-propelled tiny house, you'll need some kind of vehicle to tow your tiny house to its new location. You have a few options here. You could buy a truck, rent or borrow one, or get the professionals in by hiring a towing company to move your house for you.

Owning a truck might sound great. You could move your tiny house whenever you want! In reality, though, you probably won't move your house that often, and trucks can be expensive to buy and maintain. You might be better off using a smaller and more environmentally-friendly car for your everyday life and renting or borrowing a large truck on the few occasions that you need one.

If you'd rather not hire a company, see if you have a knowledgeable friend you could bring on board. Definitely make sure you know what you're doing too -- don't just rely on your friend! But having an experienced set of hands helping out can set you at ease and make a DIY move less stressful. When deciding which truck to rent, buy or borrow, the most important factor to consider is its towing capacity (the weight it can tow). The vehicle must be able to tow the gross weight of the house, not just what it weighed when you added up all the construction materials. Don't forget that all your living-related stuff has a weight too -- especially the water in your water tank! Typically, tiny house dwellers look for a "full-sized" truck that's rated to tow at least 10,000 pounds.

Other things to look at include suspension, cooling systems, brakes, the distance it's done, and so on. Many people prefer to tow with diesel trucks, because they tend to have a better pulling power at lower speeds. When comparing trucks, compare not just the model, but also the manufacturer and the year of manufacture.

If in doubt, err on the side of caution and go for a truck that can tow more than you need rather than one which should just about do the job. Generally, look for trucks that can tow at least 15,000 pounds and that have large engines (V-8 or V-10 should work). The sorts of trucks worth considering include the Chevrolet Silverado 2500HD, the Dodge Ram 2500, and the GMC Sierra 2500HD.

Planning the Route

Your house may be tiny as far as houses go, but it's still bigger than most of the other vehicles on the road! To ensure its safe passage, plan out your route carefully before you set off. Plot your journey so you avoid as many bends, bridges, and traffic jam hot spots as possible. Start out at a time when there's not likely to be much traffic on the roads.

Regardless of how much careful planning you do, of course, you won't be able to eliminate all potential problems before you start your move. Along the way, you may encounter bridges, phone lines, branches, overpasses, and gas station roofs that aren't high enough for your tiny house to pass underneath. Keep your eyes peeled and have a backup plan at the ready.

Once you've safely arrived at your destination, you're not quite done! You'll still need to maneuver your house into its new spot. Make sure you'll be able to access your parking space once you arrive at your destination. Arrange for someone to clear the way and measure the space ahead of time. It's also a good idea to know how you want your tiny house to be positioned, so that you can slot it straight into place.

Finally, I recommend getting a team together to help you move. As well as helping you attach your house to and detach it from the truck at the beginning and end of the journey, any friends and family you can recruit will be able to help you get your house safely to its new home. If you'll be driving the truck yourself, it's worth having someone in the passenger seat who can check your blind spot, look ahead for potential hazards, and so on. It's also worth having another car follow you. Its passengers can keep other drivers from tailgating you, stop other vehicles from getting in your way if you need to change lanes, and maybe even take photos of your tiny house on the move!

When I moved my house, I had a team of people in a chase car behind the house looking out for any potential problems. To get the house down the driveway, we had to clear several small branches from low hanging trees! You can see a video of my house being moved at www.thetinyhouse.net/moving-day

Getting Set Up

Finally, once you arrive at your destination, you'll need to detach your tiny house, make sure it's level, and connect it up to any utilities. You might also want to spend time with your new neighbors, unpack, or celebrate! If you need help with this part, check out Tiny House Decisions for my tips.

Your Address

Since tiny houses on wheels aren't permanent structures, they sadly don't get their own mailing addresses (unless they're parked on a piece of land you've purchased). Why is that an issue? Two reasons: First, you'll need some way of getting your mail. Second, you'll need to have a permanent address in order to pay your taxes and so on. Fortunately, there are a number of solutions to the first problem. The second is harder to resolve. We'll tackle the easy one first.

Enlist the Help of Friends & Family

In the case of mail, you can ask a family member or friend to receive your mail and forward it to you, drop it by every now and then, or simply keep it for you to pick up. If you know someone who's willing to do this for you, or if you live in someone's backyard or on a campsite, this may be your best bet, because it'll likely be free. However, it may get annoying for both parties fairly quickly, so make sure to clarify exactly what the agreement requires before you go this route.

If you ask someone you know to forward your mail to you, you'll need to work out how they should do this. If you mostly receive letters, using the regular postal service probably won't be too expensive. However, if you regularly receive packages, UPS or FedEx might be cheaper. You'll also need to work out a way to reimburse your friend for these costs.

Rent a PO Box or Mailbox

Your second option is to rent a PO box or a mailbox with a company like UPS. This way, all your mail will be delivered to one place and signed for, ready for you to pick up whenever is convenient. This is a simple solution, although it will cost you.

Use a Mail Forwarding Service

The third option is to use a professional mail forwarding service. These companies receive your mail for you and deliver it to you, wherever you are. They can also sort through it, scan it, shred junk, and so on. These services cost money, but they can be very hassle-free and efficient.

Speak to Your Post Office or Delivery Company

Finally, if you live in a small community, you may be able to come to an arrangement with your local post office to have your mail delivered to them or to your tiny house, even though it doesn't have a permanent address. For deliveries from other companies, you could always try describing your house in place of an address. Be prepared for some of your packages to go missing though!

Get a Permanent Address

Unfortunately, most of these solutions don't solve the problem of needing to have a permanent address for official purposes. You can't write your PO box on your tax return, for example. Pretty much your only option here is to use the address of a family member or friend as your permanent and official address.

However, before deciding which of your friends will be lucky enough to receive all of your official correspondence, it's worth finding out if it would make sense for your permanent address to be in a particular state or area. Look into insurance costs, personal income taxes, the costs of registering vehicles, and so on, to find out if you'd be financially better off "living" in one state rather than another. This is a big decision that can affect everything from where you're able to vote to how much you pay in income taxes, so make sure to do your research!

The government isn't the only organization that might have trouble with your lack of a real address. You may struggle to get contractors and other service providers to come out to your property or to install services like satellite, cable, and internet. Unfortunately, apart from pleading with the companies in question, there's not much you can do. This is where living in someone else's backyard may be an advantage, since they may already have the services you need (or at least be able to provide a landmark to help service providers find you!).

Your Neighbors

Hopefully you scoped out your new neighbors before you chose your land, but the work doesn't stop there. Neighbors are important no matter where you live, but if you're living in a tiny house -- and therefore in a legal grey area -- it's extra important that you keep them on your side.

If you don't already know your neighbors when you first move in, I'd suggest that you make the effort not only to introduce yourself, but also to explain your tiny house to them. If they seem interested, explain the tiny house movement, what tiny houses are, and why you decided to live in one. A great way to help them understand what you're doing is to show them your tiny house. Give them the grand tour or just invite them over for coffee. They'll probably be curious to see how you live in such a small space, so show them any clever space-saving tricks or other special features.

The one caveat to this approach is that if you're living under the radar, be very careful who you tell about your tiny house. Of course, close-minded folk are the least likely to support unconventional approaches like tiny house living, but bear in mind that you are technically breaking the law and that even the friendliest of people might feel the need to report you.

Whether or not they know about your style of living, stay friendly with your neighbors. Be pleasant and polite to them, and don't do anything that might annoy them, like playing loud music late at night. Should you have any problems, having your neighbors on your side could make all the difference.

What's Next?

Wherever you are on your tiny house journey, I hope you now have a much better idea about how and where to find a great spot for your tiny house! Don't forget to go back to the various sections in this book as you move forward to review all of the questions and suggestions I've posed.

The tiny house movement is growing very rapidly, and I believe that as time goes by, more cities and towns will become tiny house friendly. It's up to you and everyone else who's a part of the tiny house movement to keep moving things forward. Good luck, and keep in touch!

Part 3:
Further Reading and Resources

Tiny House Parking Stories

In the meat of *Tiny House Parking*, we focused on ideas and tips you could use to make your own tiny house parking experience as smooth as possible. I know it can be helpful to learn from other people's experiences too, though. In this section, you'll find three interviews with tiny house dwellers who typify some of the situations and strategies you just read about.

Alek Lisefksi on Living in Someone's Backyard

Please describe your tiny house.

My tiny house is an 8-by-20-foot tiny house on wheels. It's got quite a modern design with a shed-style roof and ten big windows to let in lots of light. It uses a lot of sustainable, beautiful wood and other high-end materials, so it's not an example of the cheapest tiny houses you can build. It's more of a tiny dream house.

When I first started building my tiny house, there weren't that many plans out there. I looked at all the Tumbleweed stuff and, at the time, it was all about gabled roofs. I was like, "This makes no sense to me. You're wasting so much space." There were only a couple of people that I'd even seen who were starting to do designs with the shed roof. Now it feels like every single house being built has a shed roof! It's totally becoming the norm. I don't know why it didn't take hold sooner. I guess it's because gabled roofs are cute. They make tiny houses instantly recognizable as houses and add charm to them, which isn't my style at all.

What's Sebastopol like? Is it a village or a town?

It's a town. It's pretty small. Where I live is kind of outside the city limits. It's very rural. There's open space, farmland, big backyards, and horses, and everyone has dogs.

In a sense, it's easy to find a place here. Sebastopol is a very rural spot. The town itself only has maybe seven thousand people, but the town services the entire Western Sonoma County, so there's a lot of traffic through it, even though the population itself is pretty small. It feels like a small town. On a weekday evening, you go into town and it's pretty dead. There's not a lot going on.

Describe your current tiny house location.

I'm in someone's backyard. I basically just pay rent to park my house here. They have three quarters of an acre, so there's plenty of space. I just found a little nook to park it in.

I used to do a lot more yard work and pay very little rent. But I found myself just way too busy to uphold my side of the agreement, so I offered to pay more money so they could hire someone to help out in the yard. That's the current arrangement.

How much rent do you pay?

I pay $300 a month. That includes everything. They have well water, so they don't pay for municipal water. They have solar power with a grid-type system, so they're not really paying much for electricity either. So the change in utilities for them is probably hardly noticeable.

Our original agreement was actually $50 a month, which was just to cover utilities and internet, but then I just started paying a little bit more as general rent.

What level of interaction do you have with your hosts?

I see them and say "hi" all the time, almost every day in fact, just coming and going from the house. And then occasionally I'll do something in the yard together or they'll invite me over for the holidays or for dinner. I'm kind of like part of the extended family in a way.

But I'm a little more of an introvert, so I like to have my space and privacy too. I have a pretty good mix.

Do you feel like you get the privacy you need?

Yes. I mean, I have to walk right by their house to get to my house and I share a parking area, so I'm in and out of that space together frequently. But my house is about one hundred feet away from their house and it's kind of hidden by this bush, so it feels very private once you're actually in it.

Do you have any access to your hosts' house, for laundry for example?

Yes. But my house has a combo washer/dryer, so there are very few times when I would really need anything like that. But they're really generous. If I said I couldn't fit my comforter in my washing machine and could I use theirs, they'd be like, "Sure, of course." I haven't had to do that much, but if I really needed something, they would definitely be accommodating.

How do you handle your grey water?

Right now it basically just runs onto the ground. In this location, nobody cares at all. My hosts don't care. I've asked them if I should dig a pit and build a French drain, and they're like, "What's the difference?"

Because of my location, I'm fortunate enough not to have to worry about that. Obviously if it was an urban location, it would be completely different. It's just very rural here, so it's easy. When I was building it, I didn't think I was going to find a place with a septic system -- that's why I have a composting toilet -- so I have to have another way to deal with my waste. I just assumed I could find a way to deal with grey water. I'm composting poop and I have grey water. I just assumed that would work. Unless I tried to park in the middle of San Francisco -- then that would be a problem.

Were you ever worried about addressing the issue of your composting setup in your host's yard?

No. With these people I knew it would be fine. They're a tiny bit weirded out by it, but not really.

I brought that up quite early on in the conversation. I created a page on my website and also a Craigslist ad which listed some of my requirements. One of them was a place to compost my waste. I didn't go into detail, but I made it clear from the very beginning that I needed to do that, so it wasn't super awkward. I didn't try to hide that and spring it on them later.

It's not a big deal. I don't think my hosts necessarily had any experience with it before, but after I'd been maintaining their compost box for a little while and they didn't notice any problems or smell it, they just didn't care at all. It's just not an issue because it doesn't affect them and it doesn't take up a whole lot of space.

Did you know where you were going to put the house before you started building it?

I had no clue. I didn't even know where I was going to go. When I started building it, I knew that my girlfriend at the time wanted to move out to the Bay Area for school, so I knew I'd be moving to an expensive area, and I knew it'd be great to have my own house. I just was kind of trusting that I'd find a place to park it. But I had absolutely no clue when I first started. Towards the end of the build, I started to reach out to some connections I had and to post it on Craigslist. I actually found someone a few weeks or a month before the house was done, and I negotiated a little bit. I even had a contract in place.

And three days before I left to tow the house to California, they backed out. I talked to some city supervisor and I found out that it wasn't completely legal, so they kind of freaked out and said, "We can't do this." I'd told them that before, but they must have heard something that spooked them. I honestly don't know what it was. They were just kind of like, "We're really sorry, we'd like to support you, we like the house, but we don't feel comfortable."

So when I left, I didn't have a place to park. I was on the road and every night I'd send emails. I had a couple potential spots -- a few people that I never really got back to, but who had expressed an interest in hosting me. So I got back in touch with all those people.

One of those people referred me to my current hosts. By the time I actually made it out to California, I had found a new place to park. It was just temporary, though, and I didn't even know if the house would fit back here. They were like, "You can at least just stay on our driveway for a few days until you figure it out." It turned out well, and I've been here for a year and a half now.

Did you consider any other options, besides living in someone's backyard?

I would love to live on my own land. That's definitely an option, something I want to do. But the land out here in Sonoma County costs about half a million bucks! That was never actually an option for this time in my life.

I always just thought that my house looked awesome and that it didn't take up much space, so, in a rural area, it'd be easy to find a spot. I just assumed that would work from day one.

I definitely toyed with the idea of temporarily living in an RV park if I couldn't find a more permanent place. But luckily I didn't have to do that.

I've heard that some RV parks won't accept owner-built RVs and that they need to be registered as RVs for insurance reasons. Have you heard that?

I've heard something like that. I stayed at RV parks while traveling on the way over here. All of them were totally fine with it.

I don't know if there's a difference between that and more of a permanent living situation. Maybe if you're there for a month there's some different insurance requirement? I don't know. I personally haven't experienced that, but I've also heard some rumours along those lines. That said, I also know of people who do live in RV parks full time, so I think it just varies by location.

Where did you keep the house while you were building it?

To start with, I bartered for some interior warehouse space in Ohio where I was building it. A family friend who had a manufacturing company had a huge warehouse. I just went and visited and was like, "Hey, that corner over there doesn't really look used. Do you think I could build a little house here?" He said that sounded cool. I do web design work, so he asked if I would consult with him -- talk about his website and how to improve it. I met with him occasionally, just to give him some input on things. It was a pretty simple bartering deal, where he gave me a free place to build for a few months while I got the shell built.

I started in early spring and it was really rainy, so I was so happy to have the indoor space during those spring storms, because otherwise I would have been constantly freaking out about everything getting drenched.

Once the tiny house was pretty watertight, the weather improved, and the shell was done, I brought the house outside. By then I had made a connection with this awesome woodworker who helped me do a lot of the interior finish work and who helped with some of the exterior trim work. He had a wood shop that had a fenced-in gravel parking area. So I paid the building owner a very low monthly rent to park it there for the remaining months while I finished it. It was a secure location, so I felt really good about that.

My plan was to park it in my parents' driveway to finish it, but this worked out better. Whenever the guy was there working, I was able to use his workshop, his beautiful table saw, and all his equipment. Since he was doing so much work, it was way easier for him having it there.

Did you need to make any changes to the land you're on now in order to put the tiny house there?

I didn't have to make any permanent changes, but it was actually very, very difficult. I had to do all kinds of stuff.

I had to trim back a whole line of trees. I hired someone to do all this tree trimming because they were overhanging the space and they were too low. I also had to move an entire pile of concrete blocks. I had to disassemble one of those shed kits and literally take the whole thing apart, find a new location, and put it back. I had to temporarily move a garden bed.

It was just everything actually. It turned out to be way, way more work than I had anticipated, even getting around the side of the house because the gap there is 8.5 feet exactly. The eave of the house was probably within about two inches of their house, squeaking through this corner. Everything about that maneuvering was incredibly tight. There were wires in every direction that I had to get under. It wasn't like a driveway you just pull up. It was pretty complicated. But once I actually got it here, it was great.

Do the local authorities know about your tiny house?

I don't know. I've given some open houses and I've had lots of people come to see it, so I'm not overly cautious about that. But it's also not visible from the street.

Is it visible to neighbors?

It's visible to neighbors, and I've checked in with some of them. The first couple of days I was here, I talked to some neighbors that my hosts thought might have an issue with it. I told them what I was doing and made sure they were cool.

What was that conversation like?

I walked over to the neighbour with our hosts, who said, "Hey, we're thinking of hosting this person and their tiny house. He's gonna park a tiny house in the backyard. Here's what it looks like. What do you think? Do you have any problems with this?"

The only person who expressed any concern was like, "Well, I have this nice view, so as long as you don't block my view." So I found a place to park it which was a little harder to get into but which was separated from him by some trees. It doesn't affect his view at all, so I made him happy and I just did what I needed to do.

It really is tucked away. It's just the way that the street is and how the house is already offset from the street, and how my house is behind the main house. It's really not visible. It's not like tons of people are just driving by and seeing it all day long. You really have to know it's here to find it.

Do you still have the wheels on your house? How do you have the house stabilized?

The wheels are still on it. There are some heavy jack stands in each of the corners, so it's elevated. The tires themselves aren't supporting any of the weight. They're just sort of touching the ground.

I was able to level it and then put some concrete blocks under each of those jack stands, just to provide a little firm footing underneath. In the rainy season, the ground here is actually really soft and squishy. Dealing with that really soft earth will probably be a challenge whenever I move out of here. For now, I've just compacted it underneath and created a foundation and setting for the jack stands.

That said, I was surprised after the first winter that I went through here. It rained a lot, but I haven't really releveled the house yet. Right now, one corner seems a little low and one of the jack stands isn't really supporting much weight. So I'm going to check that soon, but it's stayed pretty stable.

What advice do you have for tiny house owners who don't want to buy or who can't afford to buy land?

If you're in an urban area, it's a whole different ballgame, I think. But in my mind, if you're willing to be somewhat flexible about where you live, there are almost unlimited opportunities to find places to park.

It's such an easy thing to freak out about because you can't believe you might invest all this time into something and then not find a place to park it. But I don't know of anyone who's built a house and not found a place to park it. Some people find a place they don't necessarily love and they have to move on, but I don't know of anyone who couldn't live in their house because there's nowhere to put it.

You always find a place to park it, especially considering how much the tiny house community is growing. Assuming you have some flexibility about where you live and that you can still commute to work or whatever without it being a problem, you're going to find a place to put it.

Don't necessarily worry about exactly where it's going to go, and don't feel like you have to solve that before you start building because, if you do, you'll never start building. And even if you do find somewhere, a year later when you're done with your house, maybe that spot won't work anymore. You can't possibly plan everything that far in advance. I tell people that what I did was just trust that it'd work.

What I've learned is that the parking spot is important but your relationship with the people you're living with is even more important. You might be really picky about location and end up living with someone who's just weird and then not feel comfortable at home. That's not worth it. It's better to be in a place where you have really positive interactions with your hosts. For me, that makes all the difference.

What do you think about the legal side of living in a tiny house?

There are so many different ways to park your tiny house, but a lot of people want it to be completely legal. At the Tiny House Conference, Tammy [Strobel] and Logan [Smith] talked about finding land for your tiny house. It was all about doing what I do, which is finding someone's backyard or another place like that to put it. And people were like, "I don't want to do that. I want to put it on my own land legally," or, "I want to put it on someone else's land legally." There's no answer to that, really.

It's like people wanting these massive tiny houses that have everything in them. It's kind of missing the point of the movement. Part of adopting this lifestyle is living in a situation that may not be completely legal. That's making a statement in and of itself. A lot of people aren't comfortable with that, though.

Alek Lisefski lives in his tiny house in Sebastopol, California, about an hour north of San Francisco. You can find Alek at tiny-project.com

Hari Berzins on Working with the Authorities

Can you describe your tiny house?

It's 8 feet by 21 feet, and we built it on a flatbed trailer. We have a full sleeping loft, with two separate entrances and two separate areas to climb into, so it's like we have two bedrooms. There's a wall between the lofts to give everyone [two adults and two kids] a bit of privacy. We have a conventional toilet that hooks into our septic system. We have a three-quarters-sized bath, a shower, a little sink, and a toilet. There's lots of storage and shelves, so we can hold four wardrobes. We have a couch that we built in, and it lifts up to give us more storage.

What is your connection to the land that you live on? Do you own or rent it?

We own it because our goal was to be mortgage-free. We have three acres. We bought our land first. It cost $25,000. Then we figured out how we were going to get here [to Virginia] because we were in Florida at the time. We decided to get started there and move it up here.

When you bought the land, were there any utilities on it?

No. It was just a hillside woods with tall grass. We had to decide where the site would be, and we had the driveway put in. We saved up for a while before we moved here, so we had another chunk of money to install the well, the septic tank, and the driveway, as well as to spend on our tiny house. It took about another year before we actually moved onto the land.

How much did the rest of the site improvements cost?

We didn't need to clear any trees. I think the well, the septic, and the driveway cost about $12,000. Our tiny house also cost $12,000 in materials (we built it all ourselves).

How did you insulate your tiny house?

We used something we found on Craigslist. It was salvaged insulation -- Polyisocyanurate. It's foam and it has aluminum on the sides, so it's super insulating. I think it's the highest R-value for the thickness. We used the zip wall system, so the sheathing is airtight.

Did you ever consider any other options in terms of parking?

Because of our main intention of being mortgage-free, we already owned the land when we came across the idea of tiny houses. So we always knew our tiny house would be parked on our land and that the wheels were really only to move it from where it was built to here. I highly doubt it's ever going to move again.

So you've taken the wheels off?

Yes, the wheels are off. They're underneath it. We should probably sell them. The house is on special blocks like cinder blocks, and it's anchored down with mobile home ties. We had to have anchors every eight feet.

Where did you keep your house when you were working on it down in Florida?

In my step-dad's backyard.
Did you do most of the building there?

We started it there. We had planned to finish it there, but we got jobs up here more quickly than we expected, so we ended up moving here nine months sooner than we thought we would. When we got those jobs, we had a month to pack up and get rid of everything and to move up here. The house was framed at that point. Then we got it sheathed and closed in, so we could pull it down the road.

The majority of the building happened here, but we finished off a good part of it at the bottom of our property, where it's flat. Once we had the well, the septic, and the driveway put in, a guy with a big machine moved it into place. We needed a backhoe to pull the truck that pulled the house because it's pretty heavy. I have no idea how heavy it is because we weren't really planning on towing it anywhere.

Did you choose the town that you bought land in based on any zoning or planning rules?

We just wanted to move to this particular place and we got lucky. We were really lucky. It could have gone badly for us because we went ahead and built the house based on that early assumption that if you have a licence plate then the building inspection can't touch your zoning, which isn't true. In Virginia, any dwelling needs to be inspected and to have a certificate of occupancy or, if it's a mobile home, it has to have a stamp. They call it third party inspection, since it's not a buildings inspector but a structural engineer who gives you the stamp of approval.

Did you have to get that approval from RIVA or from another mobile home organization to get the OK for your house?

No, because our building inspector was a reasonable guy. He said that if we got a structural engineer who was licenced in the state of Virginia to say that our house met the universal state building code, he would work with us.

I had no idea how to find a structural engineer, so that took a bit of research. But we found this great guy who wrote a letter that said that our house exceeded the building code and that he only had one recommendation: one more tie down. We'd already tied it down, but he wanted us to have one more in place. So when the inspector came out, all he did was inspect that one tie down. He didn't actually come into the house.

So the structural engineer basically acted as the inspector. I think that worked well because the inspector couldn't really inspect through the wall when they were all closed up and everything, so this way he was able to cover himself (which is mainly what they need to do), by having a structural engineer who was willing to risk his license.

Obviously your tiny house has got to be sound or a structural engineer won't write a letter like that. We also had a lot of documentation, and we took pictures of everything. So when the engineer came out, he did look at everything, but it was mainly our pictures that were the big deal.

If you could go back in time and do it all over again, how would you approach it?

We tell people doing our course that you should always start with a conversation with your building department. Find out what's allowed. If you're nervous or you don't want them to know who you are, you can always just call anonymously and ask questions about what the minimum square footage is, how they would go about permitting a house on wheels, whether or not they would do that, or if it would help to have a structural engineer to inspect your build as you went along, for example.

Another thing you can do is have your own third-party inspection at each stage that you would normally have them and keep loads of documents. But I would also talk with the actual inspector based in the place where you're planning to live. That said, if you're not sure where that will be, the best thing to do would be to try and get someone like a structural engineer to do all the regular inspections and to keep your own documentation. If we had done that, it might have been even simpler.

Where I live, in Vermont, I'm having to fly under the radar, in part because bedrooms need a big egress, but the windows in my loft are not big enough to be considered egress windows. Was this a factor for you?

Because the structural engineer was our inspector, I think we got away with a lot of things that aren't exactly code. The hallway in the kitchen isn't as wide as a hallway is supposed to be, and the space either side of the toilet is not as big as the code says it should be. It's more about the spirit of the code. It was important to have a structural engineer who was able to interpret it that way and feel confident that our house was safe.

But I think these things could be issues. I have that fear too. If there was a window that we could put in, I would try to put in an egress window.

When we move out of the house, we plan to make it into a bed and breakfast and we're actually going to remodel it. We're going to take out the second loft and put a full-sized bed downstairs and have that double as the couch. And then we'll open up the loft, so that it's more like a bunk bed. If there was another place for you to sleep, you could say it was just storage space.

But yes, the loft thing is tricky because technically it's not in the code anywhere to have a ladder to a sleeping area, so even a ladder could be an issue.

Would you say it's dependent upon the building inspector you get?

It is definitely up to your local jurisdiction, so it's really important to be compliant and to seek compliance. That's why I say to start with a meeting and to work with them. They have a lot of power, so if you work with them, it's going to work better.

How do you deal with water in your house? I'm curious about how you get water into the house and whether or not you ever have issues with freezing because you're in the mountains, as I imagine it gets cold there.

It does, but we buried the line from our well to the tiny house. It's buried at the right depth, so it doesn't freeze. Where it comes out of the ground and into the house, it's covered in heat tape, so once it starts to get cold, we just turn that on.

Do you use a submerged pump for the well?

Yes, but we have a pressure tank, so we built an insulated shed. It's very insulated. In fact, probably more so than the tiny house. The shed holds our food processing equipment, all of our canned food, our washing machine, and the pressure tanks -- anything that needs to be insulated. I also use it to grow seeds, and we've actually raised chicks in there before. If it gets really cold, you can just turn on one of the plug-in radiators and just turn it to the lowest setting. It never freezes.

Do those heaters generate a lot of heat themselves?

We use an on-demand, propane, small water heater for just the washing machine. That does put out some heat. There is a freezer in the shed too, so that helps.

Is there hot water in your tiny house?

Yes. We have a 20-gallon hot water heater.

So you have two separate hot water heaters: one in the laundry room and one in the tiny house?

Yes. It is tricky because we have to time showers. We'll be like, "Is it your day for the shower?" Because there isn't really enough water for two showers, unless it's summertime and you're not using particularly hot water. But in winter there's only enough for one hot shower.

What general advice do you have for tiny house owners who want to buy their own land?

If you know you're going to build a tiny house on the land, you'll probably want to make sure that you're going to be able to live on it, so definitely check before you buy it. Check with the building and zoning departments to find out if there are restrictions of any sort on the land, whether they're deed restrictions or just zoning restrictions. Just make sure you can do what you want to do with the land. For example, if you plan to raise animals, make sure you can do that. There are some silly restrictions out there! Those things are changing though, I think.

It's hard for governments to get their heads around people wanting to build small houses on wheels. We asked our guy about building a tiny house on wheels from scratch, and he said he wouldn't let us. You'd have to have a permit to build it on a flatbed trailer and that would be hard for him, because it doesn't really fit with the rules. So we had to go the route we went and that's why some people say they'll just ask for forgiveness and that that might work better. But I don't want to tell people to do that. We just got lucky.

Do you think that if people can afford to buy land, they should build on a foundation rather than a trailer, then?

I always tell people to build on a foundation if they can, because that's straightforward. Then the only question is, "What's the smallest house you can build?" When you're building on a trailer and trying to meet all of these requirements, having just seven feet across is hard; if you had ten feet, it'd be a lot easier. I would definitely say to build on a foundation.

The other idea we had and that some friends actually did permit with the same building inspector was a house on skids. Theirs was built by a shed company. They had inspections done at the shed warehouse and then once it had been delivered and tied down properly. The inspector was fine with that. And if you ever wanted to move a house like this, it would just be moved like a shed.

Hari Berzins lives in a tiny house with her husband and two kids on their own land in Virginia. tinyhousefamily.com

Robert Whitney on Finding Land

Describe your tiny house.

My house is 98 square feet and constructed on a 7-by-14-foot trailer on top of a concrete slab. The house is heated using propane and also has electricity and well water. Although I have a composting toilet, the State of Vermont requires a septic system for greywater.

What sort of land do you live on?

My house is on a 1.1 acre lot alongside a brook. My closest year-round neighbor is about three quarters of a mile away. I own the land and was fortunate enough to buy it with a septic and well already there.

Did you have the land when you started building your tiny house?

I started building the house before buying the land and completed the purchase before the house was completed. The house was built in a friend's driveway, so I could have access to power for the tools. The plan was firm that I'd buy land for the house.

Are you pleased with your location?

I am very happy with my location. The land is on a quiet dirt road that's surrounded by woods and fields. It's limited to some degree, because cable and internet services are not possible at this time. The local library is just two to three miles away though.

I am happy at this location and will stay here until I am no longer able to live independently.

Do you have many neighbors?

There is a horse farm across the road that is presently unoccupied and up for sale. Other than that, my closest neighbor is three quarters of a mile away. People do stop in on an almost daily basis to visit.

Does your tiny house have an address?

My house has an address for 911 purposes, but as mail isn't delivered on this road, I have a box at the closest post office.

How did you find the land you currently live on?

When looking for land, the cost was of primary importance. My second priority was finding a quiet spot without neighbors or traffic.

I'd decided that I wanted to live in southern Vermont, and I connected with a real estate agent. Over two years she showed me many parcels, but they were always too expensive. I let other folks know that I was looking for land, and someone I bumped into at the post office let me know about the land that I eventually bought.

What was your land like when you first got it? Was it set up for utilities?

My land is between a brook and a dirt road, so it is longer than it is wide -- approximately 1.1 acres. There was a house on this land that had burned down a year before. A backhoe was hired to level an area for the house, connections were made to the well and septic, and a concrete "floating Alaskan" slab was poured. Electricity was brought in from a pole and put underground.

Once the house was towed in, the connections were made and I was set to occupy. I have since grown grass and planted trees. A garden will go in next.

What was the buying process like? Did you encounter any problems?

The land cost $36,000 and was paid for in cash. The process went smoothly, though patience was required. It took over two years to find and develop the land, though the house building was done in less than three months.

Buying land can be a responsibility, but it is better than renting, I think. Property taxes can be a burden. I only pay property tax on the land, not the house, as the house is considered personal and not real property.

The town knows about my house and, as long as I pay taxes, there are no problems. Winhall is a small community with a population of 700, so people are familiar, accepting, and non-judgmental.

Patience is required for anyone wishing to buy land for a tiny house. Talk to people and let others know what you want to do. People will want to help you.

What advice would you give to someone who wants to live in a tiny house? How should they go about finding some land to live on?

My advice to someone looking to live in a tiny house would be to simplify your life first. Pare down to the essentials. Try living simply first. I was in the military and was accustomed to living with few possessions and in a small space.

Before moving to a location, a person should find out from the town what's required and whether or not a tiny house is acceptable. The first piece of land I looked at was in a town that wouldn't accept a house smaller than 2,500 square feet. The second piece of land required a minimum of five acres for a house. Talk to the zoning administrator where you want to live.

Robert Whitney lives in his tiny house in Winhall, Vermont, about halfway between two ski mountains. tinyhouseparkingbook.com/robert

Tiny-Friendly Cities: The Exceptions to the Rule

As you know by now, many places are unfriendly or even hostile to tiny houses. Fortunately, a small handful of cities and towns around the country are getting out in front of any potential legal disagreements and expressly legalizing tiny houses (yay!). This just goes to show that the movement is getting the attention of the decision makers and provides examples you can bring to your local zoning officials to help make your case.

Spur, Texas

Spur is a small, rural town with a population of about 1,000. In an attempt to curb its housing crisis, the town declared itself the first tiny-house-friendly city in the US. When it saw that larger cities have done little to accommodate the pioneers of the tiny house movement, Spur removed some of its own housing size restrictions to make the town more welcoming to tiny house dwellers. There is now no minimum square footage requirement for houses in Spur.

To live in a tiny house in Spur, all you need to do is use high-quality materials, connect to the city utilities, and pay your taxes. Spur also comes with inexpensive land and a low cost of living, relatively speaking, making it ideal for the tiny house community.

Walsenburg, Colorado

In many ways, Walsenburg, Colorado is similar to Spur, Texas. In 2014, Walsenburg amended its zoning ordinance to allow tiny houses to be built in the area. Of course, there are still regulations in place that tiny house dwellers must abide by. For instance, you have to build your tiny house on a foundation or park it permanently on a footer, and you need to hook it up to the water supply and sewage system. Still, Walsenburg is friendlier to tiny houses than most cities, and it's moving in the right direction.

Portland, Oregon

Portland is often thought of as one of the most tiny-house-friendly cities out there, with its tiny house hotel and community housing projects. You can both build a structure of up to 200 square feet in Portland without getting a building permit and legally park a house on wheels. The snag is that the building code doesn't allow you to actually live in such a structure. The one loophole is if the tiny house is an accessory dwelling unit, meaning it's adjacent to a larger building (for instance, parked on the lawn of a traditionally sized house).

As I write this book, a proposal is under consideration in Portland to make tiny structures legal to live in, provided they meet certain quality standards. If the proposal is accepted and building regulations change accordingly, you'll be able to legally live in your tiny house once it's passed a habitability inspection and you've received a certificate of occupancy. The tiny house community's fingers are crossed that Portland takes this key step in living up to its reputation!

The Situation in Other Countries

The tiny house movement is slowly making its way around the globe, making tiny living a viable option for more and more people. In particular, there are now resources and communities for some European countries. While I can't possibly cover the tiny house parking situation in every single country here, let's take a brief look at a few examples.

By the way, remember that regardless of where you live, if you want to ensure that you'll be able to park your tiny house legally, talk to the relevant authorities in your area.

United Kingdom

With the tiny house movement catching on in Europe, there are now a handful of tiny house manufacturers in the UK. The movement is younger in the UK than it is in the US, though, which means there's even less information available about the legality of tiny house living there.

If your tiny house isn't going to be your permanent residence, you may be able to park it in a family member or friend's garden without too much trouble. You are allowed to live in a mobile home for twenty-eight days at a time. However, if that's not an option, you will probably need to secure planning permission in order to legally inhabit your tiny house.

Mark Burton of Tiny House UK recommends visiting your local council, armed with photos of tiny houses and a potential tiny house location, to ask for their support and guidance in building your house. To get planning permission, you'll need to complete forms, pay a fee of a couple of hundred pounds, and be prepared to wait. tinyhouseuk.co.uk/
If all else fails and you can wait a little longer, Mark is hoping to create a tiny house village where tiny house owners can live cheaply and legally. Watch this space!

France

Tiny houses, or *les petites maisons*, as they are known, are also becoming more popular in France, but, yet again, they aren't mentioned in current legislation.

To build a tiny house on private property, you need to secure permission from your local authorities. If your tiny house is portable and counts as a mobile home, you are legally allowed to stay in one place for up to three months, unless you obtain permission to stay for longer.

For more information on the legal side of tiny house parking in France, see Tiny House France (tinyhouseparkingbook.com/france) and La Tiny House (tinyhouseparkingbook.com/latinyhouse).

Germany

The tiny house movement is beginning to make its way into Germany, with pioneers such as Hanspeter Brunner at black-forest-tiny-house.com leading the way and finding ways to adapt American "Minihaus," "Mikrohaus," and "Kleinhaus" designs so that they comply with European regulations.
In Germany, as in the US, each state sets its own rules. To find out about the regulations in a particular area, it's best to speak to your local authorities. For more information about the situation in Germany more generally, read *Informationen zum Baurecht* at tinyhouseparkingbook.com/izb.

Want Help Building Your Tiny House?

Tiny House Decisions

Tiny House Decisions is a comprehensive field guide to help aspiring tiny house builders (like you) make the right choices for their unique homes. In it, I take you through the decisions I made, what I ultimately decided for my own house (and why), and how those decisions affected the overall project. I'll help you:

- Identify key choices and understand the relationships between them so you can plan your house effectively — without spending countless hours researching.
- Save hundreds or even thousands of dollars on your tiny house by avoiding common mistakes.
- Feel confident about the choices you're making, because you'll know they're the right decisions for you.

Learn more at thetinyhouse.net/tiny-house-decisions/

About the Author

Hey! I'm Ethan Waldman, the guy who wrote the book you just read. My girlfriend and I live in a 7-by-22-foot tiny house on wheels in the mountains of northern Vermont. You can read more about my story and my take on tiny house living at www.thetinyhouse.net.

Questions or comments? I'd love to hear from you! Visit thetinyhouse.net/contact to email me.

Did you enjoy this book? Please leave a review on Amazon.com. Your review will help others in the tiny house community find me! tinyhouseparkingbook.com/review will bring you directly to the review page. Thanks again!

Photo by Rikki Snyder

76951714R00047

Made in the USA
San Bernardino, CA
18 May 2018